War-Gods of t

Henry Kuttner

Alpha Editions

This edition published in 2024

ISBN 9789362922526

Design and Setting By
Alpha Editions
www.alphaedis.com
Email - info@alphaedis.com

As per information held with us this book is in Public Domain.
This book is a reproduction of an important historical work.
Alpha Editions uses the best technology to reproduce historical work
in the same manner it was first published to preserve its original nature.
Any marks or number seen are left intentionally to preserve.

Contents

I	- 1 -
II	- 9 -
III	- 17 -
IV	- 26 -
V	- 37 -

I

Earth Consul, Goodenow, tossed a packet of microfilms to Vanning, and said, "You're crazy. The man you're after isn't here. Only damn fools ever come to Venus—and don't ask me why I'm here. You're crazy to think you'll find a fugitive hiding on this planet."

Jerry Vanning, earth state investigator, moved his stocky body uneasily. He had a headache. He had had it ever since the precarious landing through the tremendous wind-maelstroms of the pea-soup Venusian atmosphere. With an effort he focused his vision on the micro-projector Goodenow handed him, and turned the tiny key. Inside the box, a face sprang into view. He sighed and slid another of the passport-films into place. He had never seen the man before.

"Routine check-up," he said patiently. "I got a tip Callahan was heading here, and we can't afford to take chances."

The consul mopped his sweating, beefy face and cursed Venusian air-conditioning units. "Who is this guy Callahan, anyway?" he asked. "I've heard a little—but we don't get much news on the frontier."

"Political refugee," Vanning said, busy with the projector. "Potentially, one of the most dangerous men in the System. Callahan started his career as a diplomat, but there wasn't enough excitement for him."

The consul fumbled with a cigar. "Can you tell me any more?"

"Well—Callahan got hold of a certain secret treaty that must be destroyed. If he shows it in the right places, he might start a revolution, particularly on Callisto. My idea is that he's hiding out till the excitement dies down—and then he'll head for Callisto."

Goodenow pursed his lips. "I see. But you won't find him here."

Vanning jerked his thumb toward a window. "The jungle—"

"Hell, no!" the consul said decidedly. "Venus, Mr. Vanning, is *not* Earth. We've got about two hundred settlements scattered here and there; the rest is swamp and mountains. When a man gets lost, we wait a few days and then write out a death certificate. Because once an Earthman leaves a settlement, his number's up."

"So?"

"So Callahan isn't here. Nobody comes here," Goodenow said bitterly.

- 1 -

"Settlers do," Vanning remarked.

"Bloody fools. They raise herbs and *mola*. If they didn't come, Venus would be uninhabited except by natives in a few years. The North-Fever ... You'd better watch out for that, by the way. If you start feeling rocky, see a doctor. Not that it'll help. But you can be put under restraint till the fever passes."

Vanning looked up. "I've heard of that. Just what—"

"Nobody knows," Goodenow said, shrugging hopelessly. "A virus. A filterable virus, presumably. Scientists have been working on it ever since Venus was colonized. It hits the natives, too. Some get it, some don't. It works the same way with Earthmen. You feel like you're cracking up—and then, suddenly—you go North. Into the swamp. You never come back. That's the end of you."

"Funny!"

"Sure it is. But—ever heard of the lemmings? Little animals that used to make mass pilgrimages, millions of them. They'd head west till they reached the ocean, and then keep going. Nobody knew the cause of that, either."

"What lies north?"

"Swamp, I suppose. How should I know? We've got no facilities for finding out. We can't fly, and expeditions say there's nothing there but the usual Venusian hell. I wish—"

"Oh-oh!" Vanning sat up, peering into the projector. "Wait a minute, Goodenow. I think—"

"Callahan? No!"

"He's disguised, but ... Lucky this is a three-dimensional movie. Let's hear his voice." Vanning touched a button on the box. A low, musical voice said:

"My name is Jerome Bentley, New York City, Earth. I'm an importer, and am on Venus to investigate the possibilities of buying a steady supply of herbs—"

"Yeah," Vanning said tonelessly. "That's it. Jerome Bentley—nuts! That's Don Callahan! He's disguised so well his own mother wouldn't know him—best make-up artist in the System. But I've studied his records till I nearly went blind and deaf. I don't make mistakes about Callahan any more."

- 2 -

Goodenow blinked. "I'll be blowed. I've seen the man a dozen times, and I'd have sworn ... well! If you're sure—"

"I'm sure." Vanning referred to the records. "Staying at the Star Palace, eh? Okay, I'll be pushing off."

"I'll go with you," the consul offered, and lifted his bulky body from behind the gleaming desk. Together the two men went out into the muggy Venusian day, which was now fading to a slow, blue dusk.

Venus did not revolve; it librated. There was no such thing as sunrise and sunset. But there was a very regular thickening and fading of the eternal cloudbanks that writhed overhead, approximating day and night. Despite the continual frantic disturbance of the atmosphere, the clouds were so thick that it was never possible to see the Sun.

Only the ragged, eye-straining movement of the grayness overhead, and the warm, humid wind that gusted against your sweating skin. And the sulphurous smells that drifted in from the jungle—odors of stagnant water and rottenness and things that grew unhealthily white.

Frontier town, Vanning thought, as he glanced around. Chicago must have looked like this, in the old days, when streets were unpaved and business was the town's only reason for existence. But Venus Landing would never grow into another Chicago. A few thousand souls, working under terrible handicaps, always fearing the North-Fever that meant death....

Muddy streets, wooden sidewalks already rotting, metal buildings, of two stories at most, long, low hydroponic sheds, a dull, hot apathy that hung over everything—that was Venus Landing. A few natives shuffled past on their snowshoe feet, looking fat and wet, as though made out of wax that had begun to run.

The Star Palace was a down-at-the-heels plastic building, stained and discolored by the damp molds. Goodenow jerked his head at the clerk.

"Where's Leester?"

"North-Fever," the man said, worrying his lower lip. "This morning ... we couldn't stop him."

"Oh, hell," the consul said hopelessly, turning to Vanning. "That's the way it is. Once the fever hits you, you go crazy. Do everything and anything to get away and head north. Leester was a nice kid. He was going back to Earth, next Christmas."

Vanning looked at the clerk. "A man named Jerome Bentley's staying here."

"He's somewhere around town. Dunno where."

"Okay," the consul said. "If he comes in, phone my office. But don't tell him we were asking."

"Yup." The clerk resumed his vague scrutiny of the ceiling. Vanning and Goodenow went out.

"Where now?"

"We'll just amble around. Hi!" The consul hailed a ricksha, drawn by a native—the usual type of vehicle in Venus Landing's muddy streets. "Hop in, Vanning."

The detective obeyed. His headache was getting worse.

They couldn't find Callahan. A few men said that they had seen him earlier that day. Someone had glimpsed him on the outskirts of the settlement.

"Heading for the jungle?" Goodenow asked quickly.

"He—yeah. He looked ... very bad."

The consul sucked in his breath. "I wonder. Let's go out that way, Vanning."

"All right. What do you figure—"

"The fever, maybe," Goodenow grunted. "It strikes fast. Especially to non-natives. If your friend Callahan's caught North-Fever, he just started walking into the swamp and forgot to stop. You can mark the case closed."

"Not till I get that treaty back," Vanning growled.

Goodenow shook his head doubtfully.

The buildings grew sparser and ceased at the edge of the pale forest. Broad-leafed jungle growths sprang from moist black soil. The ricksha stopped; the native chattered in his own tongue.

"Sure," Goodenow said, tossing him a coin. "Wait here. *Zan-t'kshan.*" His burly figure lumbered into the translucent twilight of the jungle. Vanning was at his heels.

There were footprints—many of them. The detective ignored them, moving in a straight line away from Venus Landing. Here and there were blazed *mola* trees, some with buckets hung to collect the dripping sap. The footprints grew fainter. At last only one set remained visible.

"A man. Pretty heavy-set, too. Wearing Earth shoes, not sandals like most of ours. Callahan, probably."

Vanning nodded. "He didn't come back by this route."

"He didn't come back," Goodenow said shortly. "This is a one-way trail."

"Well, I'm going after him."

"It's suicidal. But—I suppose I can't talk you out of it?"

"You can't."

"Well, come back to town and I'll find you an outfit. Supplies and a hack-knife. Maybe I can find some men willing to go with you."

"No," Vanning said. "I don't want to waste time. I'll start now." He took a few steps, and was halted by Goodenow's restraining grip.

"Hold on," the consul said, a new note in his voice. He looked closely into Vanning's face, and pursed his lips in a soundless whistle.

"You've got it," he said. "I should have noticed before."

"Got what?"

"The North-Fever, man! Now listen to me—"

Vanning's headache suddenly exploded in a fiery burst of white pain, which washed away and was gone, leaving his brain cool and ... different. It was like a—like a *cold* fever. He found his thoughts were moving with unusual clarity to a certain definite point.... North. Of course he had to go north. That was what had been wrong with him all day. He had been fighting against the urge. Now he realized that it should be obeyed, instead.

He blinked at Goodenow's heavy, worried face. "I'm all right. No fever. I want to find Callahan, that's all."

"Like hell it is," the consul said grimly. "I know the symptoms. You're coming back with me till you're well."

"No."

Goodenow made a movement as though to pinion Vanning's hands behind his back. The detective writhed free and sent a short-arm jab to Goodenow's jaw. There was power behind that blow. The consul went over backwards, his head thumping against a white tree-bole.

He lay still.

Vanning didn't look at the motionless body. He turned and began to follow Callahan's trail. But he wasn't watching the footprints. Some instinct seemed to guide him.

North ... North!

His head no longer hurt. It felt strangely cool, numb and stinging almost pleasantly. The magnetic pull drew him on. Deeper and deeper into the jungle....

Distantly he heard Goodenow's shout, but ignored it. The consul couldn't stop him. But he might try. Vanning ran for a while, lightly and easily, till the wilderness of Venus had swallowed him without trace. Then he slowed down to a walk. He would have been grateful for a brief rest, but he could not stop. Not Now....

The fog closed in. Silver mist veiled the strange, ghostly forest. Then it was torn away as a gust of wind drove down from the upper air. Above, the clouds twisted in tortured writhings; but Vanning did not look up. Not once did he turn his head. He faced north ... he plodded north ... he slogged through mushy, stinking swamp that rose at times to his waist....

A sane man would have skirted the bog. Vanning floundered across, and swam when he could no longer walk. Somewhere to the left he heard the coughing mutter of a swamp-cat's engine, but he did not see the machine. His vision was restricted to a narrow circle directly ahead.

Dimly he felt pain. The clinging, soft nettles of Venus ripped at his clothing and his skin. Leeches clung to his legs till they fell off, satiated. Vanning went on. He was a robot—an automaton.

In silence the pale forest slipped by in a fantastic procession. Lianas often made a tangled snare where Vanning fought for minutes before breaking through. Luckily, the vines had little tensile strength, but soon the man was exhausted and aching in every limb. Far above, the clouds had thickened and darkened into what passed for night on fog-shrouded Venus. But the trees gave a phosphorescent light of their own. Weird beyond imagination was the scene, with the bloody, reeling figure of the man staggering on toward the north—

North. Ever north. Until overtaxed muscles refused to bear the burden longer, and Vanning collapsed into exhausted unconsciousness.

He did not know when he awoke. Presently he found himself walking again. Nothing had changed. The jungle was denser, and the cool light from above filtered down once more. Only the light was cool. The air itself was sticky and suffocating.

He went on into hell.

Days and nights merged into a fantastic pattern of dull torture. Some distantly sane portion of his brain held back and watched, but could not help. Days and nights. There was no food. There was water, for as Vanning splashed through shallow pools he would bend his head to drink of the foul liquid. Once his feet crunched on the green-moulded bones of a human skeleton. Others had taken this way before him....

Toward the end, a fleshless, gaunt thing that had once been a man dragged itself laboriously toward a range of mountains that lifted from the swamp toward the north. They extended to left and right as far as he could see, and seemed unscalable. But they were V-shaped, and Vanning headed toward the point of the V—the inner point. The terrible drive within him drove him on relentlessly.

That night a sulphurous crimson glow lit the sky beyond the mountains. Vanning did not see it. He slept.

By morning he was on his way again, staggering into the funnel of the peaks. They were bare rock, eroded by eons of trickling water from the clouds. He could not climb them, even had he possessed the strength. He went on, instead, into the narrowing valley....

It ended in a sheer cliff of weathered stone. Vanning reeled toward the barrier. He could not return. The North-Fever drove him on remorselessly. He had to climb that wall of rock, or die. And he could not climb.

He fell, rose, and fell again. In the end he crawled. He crawled to the foot of the cliff and dragged himself upright. He fell forward, as though trying to press his body against the towering wall that lifted to the writhing grey clouds—

Fell—through the stone!

He toppled through the rock curtain as though it were non-existent! Instantly intense blackness closed around him. Hard stone was under him.

His mind was too dulled to wonder. He knew only that the way north was still open. He crept on through darkness, leaving a trail of blood behind him....

The ground dropped from under him. He crashed down on a mound of moulded vegetation.

Before the shock had passed, the living dead man was moving again. He crawled forward until his way was blocked by a perpendicular wall. Gasping dry-throated sobs, he clawed at the barrier with broken, bleeding finger-tips.

To left and right, an arm's length away, were other walls. He was in a pit. The sane part of his brain thought: "Circle around! There may be some way out!"

But Vanning could not circle. He could only move in one direction. That was north. He fumbled blindly at the wall, until unconsciousness came at last....

Twice again he awoke, each time weaker, and twice again he slept. The fever, having passed its peak, dwindled swiftly.

At last Vanning awoke, and he was sane. No longer did he feel the relentless urge to turn north. He lay for a little while staring into the blackness, realizing that he was once more in full command of his traitorous body.

There was little life left in him. His tongue was blackened and swollen till it filled his mouth. He was a scarecrow, nearly naked, his bones sharply defined through his skin.

It was an effort even to breathe. But death would not be long in coming— now....

II

Dying is an uncomfortable business, unless a man is drugged or insensible. Vanning found it so. Moreover, he wasn't the sort of man who would give up without good cause. Weak as he was, nevertheless he was still too strong to lie in the dark, waiting.

Laboriously, he got to his hands and knees and commenced a circuit of the pit. He expected nothing. But, at the southern end of his prison, he was astounded to find a hole in the wall easily large enough to admit his body.

Feeling into the blackness, he discovered the smooth floor of a passage. Good Lord! It had been there all the time, during his tortured imprisonment in the pit. If he had only searched before—

But he could not have done so, of course. Not with the North-Fever flaming in his veins.

The tunnel might lead anywhere. All the chances were against its leading to safety. Sooner or later, there would probably be a dead end. Nevertheless, there *was* a chance. That chance grew brighter as Vanning's fingers discovered that the walls bore the marks of tools.

The tunnel had been made by—perhaps not humans, but at least by some intelligent race!

It grew higher as he went on, but Vanning was too weak to rise. He realized dimly that the passage made a sharp hairpin turn.

Through the dark the distant clangor of a bell roared.

Vanning hesitated, and then resumed his weak crawl. There was nothing else to do.

The ground dropped from beneath him. He went rolling and slipping down an inclined slide, to stop with a jolt against a softly padded surface. The shock was too much for his exhausted mind and body. He felt consciousness leaving him.

But he realized that it was no longer dark. Through a pale, luminous twilight he caught a glimpse of a mask hovering over him—the mask of no human thing. Noseless save for tiny slits, gap-mouthed, round-eyed, the face was like that of a fish incredibly humanized—fantastically evolved. A patina of green scales overlaid the skin.

The gong thundered from nearby. The monstrous mask dissolved into the blackness that swept up and took Vanning to its heart. Nothing existed but pain, and that, too, was wiped out by the encompassing dark....

He was very sick. Complete exhaustion had almost killed him. He was lying on a soft pallet, and from time to time the stinging shock of a needle in his arm told him that he was being fed by injection. Later, water trickled down his throat. His swollen tongue resumed its normal shape. Sleep came, tormented by dreams. The mask of the fish-like thing swam at him from gray shimmering light. It gave place to a great bell that roared deafeningly.

Then the face of a girl, pale, lovely, with auburn ringlets clustering about her cheeks. Sympathetic blue eyes looked into his. And that, too, was gone....

He awoke to find—something—standing above him. And it was no nightmare. It was the thing of his dreams—a being that stood upright on two stocky legs, and which wore clothing, a shining silver tunic and kirtle. The head was fish-like, but the high cranium told of intelligence.

It said something in a language Vanning did not know. Weakly he shook his head. The fish-being launched into the Venusian dialect.

"You are recovered? You are strong again?"

Vanning sought for words. "I'm—all right. But where am I? Who—"

"Lysla will tell you." The creature clapped its huge hands together as it turned. The door closed behind its malformed back, opening again to reveal the auburn-haired girl Vanning recognized.

He sat up, discovering that he was in a bare room walled with gray plastic, and that he was lying on a pallet of some elastic substance. Under a metallic-looking but soft robe, he was naked. The girl, he saw, bore over her arm a bundle of garments, crimson as the kirtle she herself wore.

Her smile was wan. "Hello," she said, in English. "Feel better now?"

Vanning nodded. "Sure. But am I crazy? That thing that just went out—"

Horror darkened the girl's blue eyes. "That is one of the Swamja. They rule here."

"Here? Where's here?"

Lysla knelt beside the bed. "The end of the world—for us, Jerry Vanning."

"How do you know my name?"

- 10 -

"There were papers in your clothes—what was left of them. And—it'll be hard to explain all this. I've only been here a month myself."

Vanning rubbed his stubbly beard. "We're on Venus?"

"Yes, of course. This is a—a valley. The Swamja have lived here for ages, since before Earthmen colonized Venus."

"I never heard of them."

"None ever return from this place," Lysla said sombrely. "They become slaves of the Swamja—and in the end they die. New slaves come, as you did."

Vanning's eyes narrowed. "Hold on. I'm beginning to understand, a little. The Swamja—those fish-headed people—have a secret city here, eh? They're intelligent?"

She nodded. "They have great powers. They consider themselves the gods of Venus. You see—Jerry Vanning—they evolved long before the anthropoid stock did. Originally they were aquatic. I don't know much about that. Legends ... Anyway, a very long time ago, they built this city and have never left it since. But they need slaves. So they send out the North-Fever—"

"*What?*" Vanning's face grayed. "Lysla—what did you say? The fever's artificial?"

"Yes. The virus is carried by microscopic spores. The Swamja send it out to the upper atmosphere, and the great winds carry it all over Venus. The virus strikes very quickly. Once a man catches it, as you did, he goes north. These mountains are a trap. They're shaped like a funnel, so anyone with the fever inevitably heads into the pass, as you did. They are drawn through the mirage, which looks like a wall of rock. No one who wasn't—sick—would try to go through that cliff."

Vanning grunted, remembering. "Keep talking. I'm beginning—"

"There isn't much more. The victims fall into the pits, and stay there till the fever has run its course. The Swamja run no risks of being infected themselves. After the sickness has passed, it's easy to find the way out of the pits—and all the tunnels lead to this place."

"God!" Vanning whispered. "And you say this has been going on for centuries?"

"Very many centuries. First the natives, and now the Earthpeople as well. The Swamja need slaves—none live long here. But there is always a supply trickling in from outside."

Thousands of helpless victims, through the ages, drawn into this horrible net, dragged northward to be the slaves of an inhuman race.... Vanning licked dry lips.

"Many die," the girl said. "The Swamja want only the strongest. And only the strongest survive the trip north."

"You—" Vanning looked at Lysla questioningly.

She smiled sadly. "I'm stronger than I look, Jerry. But I almost died.... I still haven't completely recovered. I—was much prettier than I am now."

Vanning found that difficult to believe. He couldn't help grinning at the girl's very feminine admission. She flushed a little.

"Well," he said at last, "you're not Venusian, I can see that. How did you come to get sucked into this?"

"Just bad luck," Lysla told him. "A few months ago I was on top of the world, in New York. I've no parents. My father left me a trust fund, but it ran out unexpectedly. Bad investments, I suppose. So I found myself broke and needed a job. There weren't any jobs for unskilled labor, except a secretarial position in Venus Landing. I was lucky to get that."

"You've got nerve," Vanning said.

"It didn't help. The North-Fever hit me, and the next thing I knew, I was ... here. A slave."

"How many Earthmen are there here?"

"About a hundred. Not many are strong enough to reach the pass. And about the same number of Venusian natives."

"How many Swamja?"

"A thousand, more or less," Lysla explained. "Only the highest classes have slaves. Most of the Swamja are trained for the military."

"So? Who the devil do they fight?"

"Nobody. It's a tradition with them—part of their religion. They believe they're gods, and the soldiers serve as the Valkyries did in the Norse Valhalla."

"Two hundred slaves.... What weapons do the Swamja have?"

Lysla shook her head. "Not many. A paralysis hand-projector, a few others. But they're invulnerable, or nearly so. Their muscles are much tougher than ours. A different cellular construction."

Vanning pondered. He could understand that. The human heart-muscle is much stronger and tougher than—say—the biceps.

The girl broke into his thoughts. "Rebellion is quite useless. You won't believe that now, but you'll understand soon."

"Maybe," Vanning said tonelessly. "Anyhow—what's next on the program?"

"Slavery." Her voice was bitter. "Here are your clothes. When you're dressed, you'll find a ramp leading down outside the door. I'll be waiting." She detached a metal plaque from the wall and went out. Vanning, after a scowling pause, dressed and followed.

The corridor in which he found himself was of bare plastic, covered with a wavy bas-relief oddly reminiscent of water's ripples, and tinted azure and gray. Here and there cold lamps, using a principle unfamiliar to the man, were set in the walls. Radioactivity, he theorized, or the Venusian equivalent. He saw a ramp, and descended it to enter a huge low-ceilinged room, with doors at intervals set in the curving walls. One of the doors was open, and Lysla's low voice called him.

He entered a cubicle, not large, with four crude bunks arranged here and there. The girl was fitting the metal plaque into a frame over one. She smiled at him.

"Your dog-license, Jerry. You're 57-R-Mel. It means something to the Swamja, I suppose."

"Yeah?" Vanning saw a similar plaque over each of the cots. "What's this place?"

"One of the dormitories. Four to an apartment is the rule. You'll be lodged with three men who arrived a little while before you did—two Earthmen and a Venusian."

"I see. What am I supposed to do?"

"Just wait here till you're summoned. And Jerry—" She came toward him, placing her palms flat on his broad chest, her blue eyes looking up into his appealingly. "Jerry, please don't do anything foolish. I know it's hard at first. But—*they*—punish rebellious slaves rather awfully."

Vanning smiled down at her. "Okay, Lysla. I'll look around before I do anything. But, believe me, I intend to start a private little revolution around here."

She shook her head hopelessly, auburn curls flying. "It isn't any use. I've seen that already. You'll see it, too. I must go now. And be careful, Jerry."

He squeezed her arm reassuringly. "Sure. I'll see you again?"

"Yes. But now—"

She was gone. Vanning whistled softly, and turned to examine the room. Sight of his face in a mirror startled him. Under the stubbly growth of beard, his familiar features had altered, grown haggard and strained.

A razor lay handy—or, rather, a sharp dagger with a razor-sharp edge. There was a bar of gray substance that gave a great deal of lather when Vanning moistened it in the metal bowl that served as a wash-basin. He shaved, and felt much better.

His weakness had almost entirely gone. The medical science of the Swamja, at least, was above reproach. Nevertheless, he tired easily.... That would pass.

Who were his bunk-mates in this cubicle? Idly Vanning scrutinized their effects, strewn helter-skelter on the shelves. Nothing there to tell him. There was a metal comb, however, and Vanning reached for it. It slipped from his fingers and clattered to the plastic floor.

Vanning grunted and got down on his knees to recover the object, which had skidded into a dark recess under the lowest shelf. His fumbling fingers encountered something cold and hard, and he drew it out wonderingly. It was a flat case, without ornament, and clicked open in his hands.

It was a make-up kit. Small as it was, it contained an incredible quantity of material for disguises. Tiny pellets were there, each stamped with a number. Dyestuffs that would mix with water. There was a package of *isoflex*, the transparent, extraordinary thin "rigid cellophane" of the day. There were other things....

Vanning's eyes widened. Two and two made an unmistakable four. Only one man on Venus would have reason to possess such a kit. That man was Don Callahan, whom Vanning had vainly pursued from Mars to Earth, and thence to Venus.

Callahan here!

But why not? He, too, had fallen victim to North-Fever. He had simply preceded Vanning in his drugged trip to this hidden kingdom.

"Who the hell are you?"

The harsh question brought Vanning to his feet, instinctively concealing the make-up kit in his garments. He stared at the man standing on the threshold—a husky, broad-shouldered specimen with flaming red hair and a scarred, ugly face. Squinting, keen eyes watched Vanning.

"I'm—your new room-mate, I guess," the detective said tentatively. "Jerry Vanning's my name."

"Mine's Sanderson. Kenesaw Sanderson." The other rubbed a broken nose thoughtfully. "So you're new. Well, get this straight. Don't try any tricks with the Swamja or get any ideas."

Vanning tilted his head to one side. "I don't get it."

"New guys," Sanderson said scornfully. "They're always figuring it'll be easy to escape. They try it, and we all suffer. The Swamja are tough babies. Take it easy, do what you're told, and everything's okay. See?"

"Not quite." There was a roughness in Vanning's tone. "How long have you been here?"

"A few weeks, about. I don't recall exactly. What of it?"

"You don't look yellow. It just seems funny that you'd give up so easily. You look pretty tough."

Sanderson snarled deep in his throat. "I am tough! I'm also smart. Listen, Mr. Jerry Vanning, two days after I got here I saw the Swamja punish a guy who tried to escape. They skinned him alive! You hear that? And his bunk-mates—they weren't killed, but one of 'em went crazy. Those Swamja—it's crazy to try and buck them."

"They've got you out-bluffed already, eh?"

Sanderson strode forward and gripped Vanning's shoulder in a bruising clutch. "You talk too much. Trouble-makers don't go here. Get that through your head."

Vanning said gently, "Let go of me, quick. Or—"

"Let him go, Kenesaw," a new voice broke in. Sanderson grunted, but released the detective. He nodded toward the door.

"Got off early, eh, Hobbs?"

"A little." The man in the doorway was as big as Sanderson, but his face was benevolent, gentle, and seamed with care. White hair bristled in a ruff above his broad forehead. "A little," he repeated. "Zeeth and I must go back tonight for the festival."

"*Sta.* We must go back tonight," said Zeeth, in the Venusian dialect. He appeared from behind Hobbs, a native of Venus, with the familiar soft plumpness and huge feet of the race. His dog-like eyes examined Vanning. "New?"

The detective introduced himself. He was secretly puzzled. One of these three men, apparently, was Callahan—but which one? None of them resembled the man Vanning had seen on the micro-projector back at Venus Landing. But, still—

III

On impulse, Vanning took out the make-up kit and held it up. "I found this under the shelves. Yours, Hobbs? Or Sanderson?"

Both men shook their heads, frowning. Vanning glanced at the Venusian.

"Yours, Zeeth?"

"*Esta*, it is not mine. What is it?"

"Just a case." Vanning stowed it away, and sat down on one of the cots, wondering. As he saw it, he had two objectives to reach. First—escape. Second—bring in Callahan.

Not merely escape, though. He thought of Lysla. A slave ... *damn*! And the other two hundred slaves of the Swamja ... He couldn't leave them here.

But what could he do? Conquer the Swamja? The thought was melodramatically crazy. Perhaps alone he might contrive to escape, and bring a troop of Space Patrolmen to wipe out the Swamja. An army, if necessary.

The others, he saw, had seated themselves on the cots. Hobbs kicked off his sandals and sighed. "Wish I had a smoke. Oh, well."

Vanning said sharply, "Callahan!" His eyes flicked from one to another, and found nothing but surprise in the faces turned to him. Sanderson rumbled,

"What the devil are you jabbering about?"

Vanning sighed. "I'm wondering something. When did you boys get here?"

It was the mild-faced Hobbs who answered. "A couple of weeks ago, I believe. Within a few days of each other. Just before you arrived, in fact. But we recovered long before you did. It was only a miracle that saved your life, Vanning."

"And before you three got here—any others come from outside? Lately, I mean."

"Not for months," Hobbs answered. "So I heard. Why?"

"Why? It proves that one of you is the man I'm after—Don Callahan. I'm a detective; I came to Venus to find Callahan, and—by accident—I followed him here. It stands to reason that one of you is the man I want."

Sanderson grinned. "Don't you know what the guy looks like?"

- 17 -

"No," Vanning admitted. "I've recognized him before by certain tricks he's got—the way he walks, the way he jerks his head around suddenly. Before he came to Venus, I found out, he went to an anthro-surgeon and got remodeled. A complete new chassis, face and body complete. Even got skin-grafts on his finger-tips. In time the old prints will grow back, but not for months. Meantime, Callahan's pretty well disguised."

"Good Lord!" Hobbs said. "One of us—"

Vanning nodded. "When he came to Venus, he put a disguise over his new, remodeled face. That's gone now, of course. One of you three is Callahan."

Zeeth, the Venusian native, said softly, "I do not think the usual laws hold good here."

Sanderson roared with laughter. "Damn right! You expect to arrest your man and ask the Swamja to imprison him for you?"

Vanning shook his head, smiling crookedly. "Scarcely. I'm getting out of this place sooner or later, and Callahan's going with me. Later, I'll bring back troops and clean out the Swamja. But I'm not forgetting about Callahan."

Hobbs shrugged. "It isn't me."

"Nor me," Zeeth said. Sanderson only grinned.

Vanning grunted. "It's one of you. I'm pretty sure of that. And I'm talking to you now, Callahan. You'll be able to disguise your walk and your mannerisms, and I can't recognize your new face or fingerprints. But sooner or later you'll forget and betray yourself. Then I'll have to take you back to Earth."

"You will forget," Zeeth said. "In a year—five, if you live, you will forget. Our people have legends of this land, where the gods live. Our priests taught that the North-Fever is sent by the gods. We did not know how true that teaching was...." His bulbous face was grotesque in its solemnity.

Vanning didn't answer. His hope of tricking an admission from Callahan had failed. Well, there would be time enough. Yet obviously one of these three was the fugitive. Hobbs? Sanderson? Certainly not Zeeth—

Wait a bit! Suppose Callahan had disguised himself as a Venusian native? That would be a perfect masquerade. And the diabolical skill of the anthro-surgeon could have transformed Callahan into a Venusian.

Vanning looked at Zeeth with new interest. The native met his glance with stolid calm.

- 18 -

"One cannot argue with fate. Those who died on the way here are luckier. We must live and serve."

"I've got other ideas," the detective growled.

Zeeth gestured vividly. "Your race does not accept destiny, as ours does. We have from birth a struggle for existence. Venus is a hard mistress. But some of us live. Yet even then there is the shadow of the North-Fever. At any time, we know, the sickness may fall upon us. If it does, and we are not kept close prisoners, we go into the jungle and either die or—come here. My brother was very lucky. He had the fever three years ago, but I held him and called for help. My tribesmen came running and tied Gharza tightly, so that he could not escape. For ten days and nights the fever made him mad. Then it passed. The threat had left him forever. The North-Fever only strikes once, so Gharza was immune. I, too, am immune—but I consider myself dead, of course."

"Aw, shut up," Sanderson snapped. "You give me the leapin' creeps. Let's get some sleep. We've got to attend the festival tonight."

"What's that?" Vanning asked.

The mild-faced Hobbs answered him. "A religious ceremony. Just do what you're told, and you'll be all right."

"Just that, eh?"

"Our people have learned to bow our heads to Fate," Zeeth murmured. "We are not fighters. Pain is horrible to us. You call us cowards. From your standards, that is true. Only by bowing to the great winds have we managed to survive."

"Shut up and let me sleep," Sanderson ordered, and relaxed his heavy body on a bunk. The others followed his example, all but Vanning, who sat silently thinking as hour after hour dragged past.

The door opened at last, and a Swamja stood on the threshold. He wore the familiar costume of the race, but there was an oddly-shaped gun in a holster at his side.

"Time!" he barked in the Venusian dialect. "Hasten! You—" He pointed to Vanning. "Follow me. The others know where to go."

The detective silently rose and followed the Swamja into the huge room. It was filled now, he saw, with natives and with Earthmen, hurrying here and there like disturbed ants. There were no other Swamja, however.

One of the Venusians stumbled and fell. He was a thin, haggard specimen of his species, and how he had ever survived the trip north Vanning could

- 19 -

not guess. Perhaps he had been in this lost city for years, and had been drained of his vitality by weeks of arduous servitude. He fell....

The Swamja barked a harsh command. The native gasped a response, tried to rise—and failed.

Instantly the Swamja drew his gun and fired. The Venusian collapsed and lay still. Vanning took a step forward, hot with fury, to find himself drawn back by Hobbs' restraining hand.

"Easy!" the other whispered. "He's dead. No use—"

"Dead? I didn't hear any explosion."

"You wouldn't. That gun fires a charge of pure force that disrupts the nervous system. It was set to kill just now."

The Swamja turned. "I must attend to this carcass. My report must be made. You, Zeeth—take the new slave to Ombara."

"I obey." The native bowed and touched Vanning's arm. "Come with me."

Followed by Sanderson's sardonic grin, Vanning accompanied the Venusian into a corridor, and up a winding spiral ramp. He found it difficult to contain himself.

"Good God!" he burst out finally. "Do those devils do that all the time? Plain cold-blooded murder?"

Zeeth nodded. "They have no emotions, you see. They are what you call hedonists. And they are gods. We are like animals to them. The moment we make a mistake, or are no longer useful, we are killed."

"And you submit to it!"

"There was a rebellion two years ago, I heard. Twenty slaves died to every Swamja. They are like reptiles—nearly invulnerable. And we have no weapons, of course."

"Can't you get any?"

"No. Nor would I try. Venusians cannot endure pain, you understand. To us, pain is worse than death."

Vanning grunted, and was silent as they passed through a curtained arch. Never would he forget his first sight of the Swamja city. It was like—

Like an ocean world!

He stood upon a balcony high over the city, and looked out at a vast valley three miles in diameter, scooped out of the heart of the mountains as though by a cosmic cup. Overhead was no sky. A shell of transparent substance made a ceiling above the city, a tremendous dome that couched on the mountain peaks all around.

Gray-green light filtered through it. An emerald twilight hazed the fantastic city, where twisted buildings like grottos of coral rose in strange patterns. It was a labyrinth. And it was—lovely beyond all imagination.

"Those—things—built this?" Vanning breathed.

"They knew beauty," Zeeth said. "They have certain senses we do not have. You will see...."

From the exact center of the city a tower rose, smooth and shining as metal. It reached to the transparent dome and seemed to rise above it, into the clouds of Venus.

"What's that?" Vanning asked, pointing. "Their temple?"

Zeeth's voice held irony. "Not a temple—a trap. It is the tube through which they blast the spores of the North-Fever into the sky. Day and night without pause the virus is blown upward through that tube, far into the air, where it is carried all over the planet."

The air was darkening, thickening. Here and there rainbow lights sprang into view. Elfin fires in an enchanted world, Vanning thought.

Through the grotesque city equally grotesque figures moved, to be lost in the shadows. The monsters who ruled here—ruled like soulless devils rather than gods.

"Come. We must hurry." Zeeth tugged at Vanning's arm.

Together they went down the ramp into one of the winding avenues. It grew darker, and more lights came on. Once Vanning paused at sight of a corroded metal structure in the center of a well-lighted park.

"Zeeth! That's a space-ship! A light life-boat—"

The Venusian nodded. "And it is well guarded, too. It crashed through the dome a century ago, I was told. All the men in it were killed. A space-wreck, I suppose."

Vanning was silent as they went on. He was visualizing what had happened in that distant past. A wreck in space, a few survivors taking to this life-boat and setting out, hopelessly, for the nearest world—believing, perhaps, that if they reached Venus, they would be saved. And then the tremendous

- 21 -

atmospheric tides and whirlpools of the clouded planet, in which no aircraft but the hugest could survive....

Vanning whistled softly. Suppose he managed to get into that space-boat? Suppose there was still rocket-fuel in the tanks, and suppose it hadn't deteriorated? Couldn't he blast up through the dome to freedom?

Sure—to freedom and death! No ship could survive in the Venusian atmosphere, certainly not this light space-tub, of an antiquated and obsolete design.

At one of the twisted buildings, Zeeth paused. The structure was larger than Vanning had imagined from above, and his eyes widened as he followed the Venusian up winding ramps, past curtained arches, till at last they stepped into a luxurious chamber at the top. Seated on a low tussock was a Swamja, fat and hideous, his bulging eyes glaring at the intruders.

"You are late," he said. "Why is that?"

Zeeth bowed. "We came as swiftly as possible."

"That may be. And this slave is new. Yet errors are not permitted. For your mistake, this—" A malformed hand rose, clutching a gun. "And this."

Instinctively Vanning tensed to leap forward, but a blast of searing fire seemed to explode in his body. He dropped in a boneless huddle, gasping for breath. Beside him he saw Zeeth, similarly helpless, fat face twisted in agony. Venusians, Vanning remembered, were horribly sensitive to pain; and even through his own torture he felt anger at the Swamja for meting out such ruthless justice.

But it was over in a moment, though that moment seemed to last for eternities. Zeeth stood up, bowed again, and slipped from the room, with a warning glance at Vanning, who also rose.

The Swamja raised his gross body. "Carry this tray. This flask and goblet— for my thirst. This atomizer—to spray on my face when I demand it. This fan for the heat."

Vanning silently picked up the heavy metal tray and followed the lumbering, monstrous figure out. He had an impulse to bring the tray down on the Swamja's head. But that wouldn't solve anything. He'd have to wait—for a while, anyway. A show of temper might cost him his life.

Along the twisting avenue they went, and to a many-tiered amphitheatre, where the Swamja found a seat in a cushioned throne. Already the place was filled with the monsters. Many of them were attended by human or

Venusian slaves, Vanning saw. He stood behind the Swamja, ready for anything, and looked down.

In the center of the pit was a pool. It was perhaps ten feet square, and blackly opaque. That was all.

"The spray."

Vanning used the atomizer on the scaly face of his master. Then he looked around once more.

Not far away, standing behind another Swamja, was Sanderson. The red-haired man met his eye and grinned mockingly.

Neither Hobbs nor Zeeth was visible. But Vanning could not repress a feeling of pleasure as he saw, several tiers down, the slim figure of Lysla, her auburn curls bare in the cool night air, a tray similar to his own held strapped to her slender neck.

Vanning's pleasure was lost in resentment. Damn these fish-headed Swamja!

"Fool!" a croaking voice said. "Twice I have had to demand the spray. Put down your tray."

Vanning caught himself and obeyed. The Swamja turned and leveled his gun. Again the blazing, brief agony whirled sickeningly through the detective's body.

It passed; silently he resumed his task. From time to time, he tended to the Swamja's wants. But he also found time to glance at Lysla occasionally.

When the ceremony began, Vanning could not tell. He sensed that the assembly had grown tenser, and noticed that the eye of every Swamja was focused on the black pool. But there was nothing else. Silence, and the deformed figures staring at the jet square in the center.

Was this all? It seemed so, after half an hour had passed. Not once had the Swamja he tended demanded attention. What the devil were the creatures seeing in that pool?

For they saw something, Vanning was certain of that. Once a shiver of pure ecstasy rippled through the Swamja's gross body. And once Vanning thought he heard a musical note, almost above the pitch of audibility. It was gone instantly.

Zeeth had said that the Swamja possessed other senses than those of humans. Perhaps those strange senses were being used now. He did not know then, nor was he ever to know, the non-human psychology of the Swamja, or the purpose of the black pool. Yet Vanning unmistakably sensed that here was something above and beyond the limitations of his own humanity.

He grew tired, shifting from foot to foot, but it seemed the ceremony would never end. He watched Lysla. Thus he saw her bend forward with a filled goblet—and, losing her balance, spill the liquid contents into the lap of the Swamja she tended.

Instantly she shrank back, her tray clattering to the floor. Stark panic fear was in her posture as she cowered there. There was reason. The Swamja was rising, turning, and in his huge hand was a gun....

He was going to kill Lysla. Vanning knew that. Already he was familiar with the Swamja code that did not forgive errors. And as he saw the stubby finger tightening on the trigger-button, Vanning acted with swift, unthinking accuracy.

His hand closed over the flask on his tray, and he threw it unerringly. The fragile substance crashed into the face of the Swamja menacing Lysla, shattering into glittering shards. The being blinked and pawed at its eyes. In a moment—

Vanning jumped clear over his own Swamja and hurtled down the steps. His shoulder drove into the blinking monster beneath Lysla, and sent the creature head-over-heels into the lap of another of its race below. Vanning caught up the gun the Swamja had dropped. He turned to look into Lysla's frightened eyes.

"Jerry—" Her voice was choked. "Oh, no!"

Abruptly a crash sounded from above. Vanning looked up to see Sanderson swinging his metal tray like a maniac. The man's red hair was like a beacon in the strange light. He drove his weapon into the snarling face of a Swamja and yelled down at Vanning:

"Amscray! There's an oorday on your eftlay!"

Pig-Latin! A door on the left? Vanning saw it. With one hand he caught Lysla's arm, and with the other smashed the gun-butt viciously into the mask of a Swamja that rose up before him.

The creature did not go down. Its arms closed about Vanning. He reversed the gun and squeezed the trigger-button, but without result. Apparently the things were immune to their own weapons.

The amphitheatre was in an uproar. In a flashing glance Vanning noticed that the black pool far below was curiously disturbed. That didn't matter. What mattered was the devil that was seeking to break his back—

Lysla tore the gun from Vanning's hand, firing it twice. The gnarled arms relaxed. But the two humans were almost hemmed in by the aroused Swamjas.

A burly body dived into the mob, followed by another one. Hobbs yelled, "Come on, kid! Fast!"

Hobbs and Zeeth! They, too, had come to the rescue. And none too soon!

The unexpected assault broke the ranks of the Swamja for an instant, and then the Earth-people were through, racing down a slanting corridor. They emerged outside the amphitheatre. Lysla gave them no time to rest. Footsteps were thudding behind them.

"This way. They'll kill us now if they catch us."

She sped into an alleyway that gaped nearby. Vanning saw Hobbs and Sanderson racing in pursuit. So Sanderson had got through, too. Good!

Zeeth?

The Venusian reeled against Vanning, his fat face contorted. "I'm—hit. Go on—don't mind me—"

"Nuts," the detective growled, and hoisted the flabby body to his shoulder. Zeeth had more courage than any of them, he thought. Weak of physique, hating pain, yet he had not hesitated to join his companions in a hopeless battle....

IV

Vanning sped after the others, who had waited for him. After that it was a desperate hare-and-hounds chase, with Lysla leading them through the labyrinth of the city, her slender legs flying.

"You okay?" Vanning gasped as he ran shoulder to shoulder with the girl for a moment.

Her white teeth were fixed in her lower lip. "I ... I shot at that Swamja's eyes. Blinded him. It's the only way ... *ugh*!"

"Where now?" Hobbs panted, his white hair rippling with the wind of his racing. Sanderson echoed the question.

"Lysla? Can we—"

"I don't know. We've been heading north. Never been there before. Can't go south—gates are always guarded."

Hobbs panted, "There are only two ways out. The way we came in—guarded, eh?—and another gate at the north."

"We'll try it," Vanning said. "Unless we can get to that space-ship—"

Zeeth wriggled free. "Put me down. I'm all right now. The space-ship—that's guarded too. But there aren't any soldiers at the north gate. I don't know why."

Through the city a rising tumult was growing. Lights were blazing here and there, but the party kept to the shadows. Twice they flattened themselves against walls as Swamja hurried past. Luck was with them; but how long it would last there was no way of knowing.

Suddenly a great voice boomed out, carrying to every corner of the city. It seemed to come from the dome high above.

"Attention! No slaves will be permitted on the streets unless accompanied by a Swamja master! No quarter is to be given to the fugitives who blinded a guard! Capture them alive if possible—they must serve as an example. But show them no quarter!"

Lysla's face had paled. Vanning glanced at her, but said nothing. Things were bad enough as they were. Only Sanderson chuckled sardonically.

"Nice going, Vanning. How about Callahan now?"

- 26 -

The detective grunted. Zeeth panted, "I would—have preferred a—peaceful death. I do not—like torture."

Vanning felt a pang of sympathy for the fat little native. But he couldn't help him. Escape was the only chance.

"Here," Lysla gasped, pausing in the shadow of a tall building. "These outer houses are all deserted. There's the gate."

Across a dim expanse of bare soil it loomed, a wall of metal rising high above their heads. Vanning stared.

"No guards. Maybe it's locked. Still ... I'm going out there. If there are any Swamja, they'll jump me. Then run like hell. Don't try to help."

Without waiting for an answer he sprinted across the clearing. At the door he paused, staring around. Nothing stirred. He heard nothing but the distant tumult from within the city. Looking back, he could see the faint elfin-lights glowing here and there, and the shining tube rising to the dome—the tube that was pouring out the North-Fever virus into the atmosphere of tortured, enslaved Venus.

And these were the gods of Venus, Vanning thought bitterly. Devils, rather!

He turned to the door. The locks were in plain sight, and yielded after a minute or two to his trained hands. The door swung open automatically.

Beyond was an empty, lighted tunnel, stretching bare and silent for perhaps fifty yards. At its end was another door.

Vanning held up his hand. "Wait a bit!" he called softly. "I'll open the other one. Then come running!"

"Right!" Sanderson's voice called back.

An eternity later the second door swung open. Vanning gave the signal, and heard the thud of racing feet. He didn't turn. He was staring out across the threshold, a sick hopelessness tugging at his stomach.

The door to freedom had opened—mockingly. Ahead of him was the floor of a canyon, widening as it ran on. But the solid ground existed for only a quarter of a mile beyond the threshold.

Beyond that was flame.

Red, crawling fire carpeted the valley from unscalable wall to granite scarp. Lava, restless, seething, boiled hotly down the slope, reddening the low-hanging fog into scarlet, twisting veils. Nothing alive could pass that terrible barrier. That was obvious.

Zeeth said softly, "It will be a quicker death than the Swamja will give us."

"No!" Vanning's response was instinctive. "Damned if I'll go out that way. Or let—" He stopped, glancing at Lysla. Her blue eyes were curiously calm.

"The cliffs?" she suggested.

Vanning scanned them. "No use. They can't be climbed. No wonder the Swamja left this door unguarded!"

"Wonder why they had it in the first place?" Hobbs asked.

"Maybe there was a way out here once. Then the lava burst through ... I've seen lava pits like this on Venus," Sanderson grunted. "They're pure hell. This isn't an exit—except for a salamander."

"Then there's no way?" Lysla asked.

Vanning's jaw set. "There's a way. A crazy way—but I can't see any other, unless we can get out by the south gate."

"Impossible," Hobbs said flatly.

"Yeah. They'll have plenty of guards there now ... I mean the space-ship."

There was a momentary silence. Zeeth shook his head.

"No ship can live in the air of Venus."

"I said it was a crazy way. But we might get through. We just might. And it's the only chance we have."

Sanderson scratched his red head. "I'm for it. I don't want to be skinned alive ... I'm with you, Vanning. You a pilot?"

"Yeah."

"You'll have to be the best damned pilot in the System to get us through alive."

Lysla said, "Okay. What are we waiting for?" An indomitable grin flashed in her grimy, lovely face.

"Good girl," Hobbs encouraged. "We'd better get out of here, anyway. Back to the city."

They returned through the valve, without troubling to close the doors. "The Swamja might think we tried to get through the lava," Vanning explained. "We need all the false trails we can lay. Now—we'd better hide out for a bit till the riot dies down."

"Good idea," Sanderson nodded.

- 28 -

"These outer buildings are deserted—I told you that. We can find a hiding-place—"

Lysla led them into one of the structures, and into a room below the level of the street. "They'll search, but it'll take a while. Now I suppose we just wait."

Since there were no windows, the light Lysla turned on would not attract attention. Nevertheless, Vanning subconsciously felt the urge to remain in darkness.

He grinned mirthlessly. "I'm beginning to know how you feel, Callahan. Being a fugitive must be pretty tough."

Nobody answered.

The silence ran on and on interminably. Finally Sanderson broke it.

"We forgot one thing. No slaves are allowed on the streets tonight without a Swamja along."

"I didn't forget," Lysla said in a low voice. "There wasn't any other way."

"But we haven't a chance in the world to get through."

"I know that, too," the girl whispered. "But—" Abruptly she collapsed in a heap, her auburn curls shrouding her face. Under the red tunic her slim shoulders shook convulsively.

Sanderson took a deep breath. A wry smile twisted his mouth.

"Okay, Vanning," he said. "Let's have that make-up kit."

The detective stared. Curiously, he felt no exultation. Instead, there was a sick depression at the thought that Sanderson—the man who had fought at his side—was Callahan.

"I don't—"

Sanderson—or Callahan—shrugged impatiently. "Let's have it. This is the only way left. I wouldn't have given myself away if it hadn't been necessary. You'd never have suspected me ... let's have it!"

Silently Vanning handed over the make-up kit. Lysla had lifted her head to watch Callahan out of wondering eyes. Hobbs was chewing his lip, scowling in amazement. Zeeth was the only one who did not look surprised.

But even he lost his impassivity when Callahan began to use the make-up kit. It was a Pandora's box, and it seemed incredible that a complete disguise could issue from that small container. And yet—

Callahan used the polished back of it as a mirror. He sent Lysla for water and containers, easily procurable elsewhere in the building, and mixed a greenish paste which he applied to his skin. Tiny wire gadgets expanded his mouth to a gaping slit. Artificial tissue built up his face till his nose had vanished. *Isoflex* was cut and moulded into duplicates of the Swamja's bulging, glassy eyes. Callahan's fingers flew. He mixed, painted, worked unerringly. He even altered the color of his garments by dousing them in a dye-solution, till they had lost the betraying red tint that betokened a slave.

In the end—a Swamja stood facing Vanning!

"All right," Callahan said tiredly. "I'll pass—if we keep out of bright lights. Now go out and help Lysla do guard duty. I'm going to disguise you all. That'll help."

Vanning didn't move as the others left. Callahan took an oilskin packet from his belt and held it out. "Here's the treaty. I suppose you came after that."

The detective opened the bundle and checked its contents. He nodded. It was the vital treaty, which would have caused revolution on Callisto. Slowly Vanning tore it into tiny shreds, his eyes on Callahan. It was difficult, somehow, for him to find words.

The other man shrugged. "That's that. And I suppose you'll be taking me back to Earth—if we get out of this alive."

"Yeah," Vanning said tonelessly.

"Okay." Callahan's voice was tired. "Let's go. We haven't time to disguise everybody—that was just an excuse to give you the treaty. A private matter—"

He shuffled to the door, with the lumbering tread of the Swamja, and Vanning followed close at his heels.

The others were waiting.

Vanning said, "Okay. Let's start. No time to disguise ourselves. Stay behind—"

In a close group the five moved along the avenue, Callahan in the lead.

The outlaw's disguise was almost perfect, but nevertheless he did not trust to it entirely. When possible, he moved along dimly-lighted streets, the four others keeping close to his heels. Once a patrol of Swamja guards passed, but at a distance.

"I'm worried," Callahan whispered to Vanning. "Those creatures have—different senses from ours. I've a hunch they communicate partly by telepathy. If they try that on me—"

"Hurry," the detective urged, with a sidewise glance at Lysla. "And for God's sake don't get lost."

"I won't. I'm heading for the left of the tube-tower. That's right, isn't it?"

Zeeth nodded. "That's it. I'll tell you if I go wrong. Careful!"

A Swamja was waddling toward them. Callahan hastily turned into a side street, making a detour to avoid the monster. For a while they were safe....

Lysla pressed close to Vanning, and he squeezed her arm reassuringly, with a confidence he could not feel. Not until now had he realized the vital importance of environment. On Mars or barren Callisto he had never felt this helplessness in the face of tremendous, inhuman powers—against which it was impossible to fight. Hopeless odds!

But luck incredibly favored them. They reached their destination without an alarm being raised. Crouching in the shadows by the square where the space-ship lay, they peered at the three guards who paced about, armed and ready.

"Only three," Lysla said.

Vanning chewed at his lip. "Callahan, you know more about locks than I do. When we rush, get around to the other side of the ship and unlock the port. It may not be easy. The rest of us—we'll keep the Swamja busy."

Callahan nodded. "I suppose that's best. We've only one gun."

"Well—that can't be helped. Lysla, you go with Callahan."

The blue eyes blazed. "No! It'll take all of us to manage the guards. I'm fighting with you."

Vanning grunted. "Well—here. Take the gun. Use it when you get a chance, but be careful. Zeeth? Hobbs? Ready?"

The two men nodded silently. With a hard grin on his tired face, Vanning gave the signal and followed the disguised Callahan as he walked toward the ship. Maybe the guards wouldn't take alarm at sight of one of their own race, as they thought. But the masquerade couldn't keep up indefinitely.

The sentries looked toward the newcomers, but made no hostile move. One of them barked a question. Callahan didn't answer. He kept lumbering toward the ship, his masked face hideous and impassive. Vanning, at his heels, was tense as wire. Beside him, he heard Zeeth breathing in little gasps.

Twenty paces separated the two parties—fifteen—ten. A guard croaked warning. His hand lifted, a gun gripped in the malformed fingers.

Simultaneously Lysla whipped up her weapon and fired. Once—twice—and the Swamja cried out and dropped his gun, pawing at his eyes. Then—

"Let 'em have it!" Vanning snarled—and sprang forward. "Callahan! Get that port open!"

The masked figure hesitated, gave a whispered sound that might have been a curse, and then sprinted around the side of the space-ship. Vanning didn't see him. His shoulder caromed into the middle of the second guard, and the two went down together, slugging, clawing, kicking.

The Swamja was incredibly strong. His mouth gaped at Vanning's throat. With an agile twist, the detective wrenched himself away, but by that time there was a gun leveled at his head. A wave of blazing agony blasted through Vanning's body—and was instantly gone. The weapon had not been turned up to the killing power.

The Swamja twisted the barrel with one finger, making the necessary adjustment. But Vanning hadn't been idle. His hands crossed over the gun, wrenched savagely. There was a crack of breaking bone, and the Swamja croaked in agony, his fingers broken.

He wasn't conquered—no! Ignoring what must have been sickening pain, he threw his arms around Vanning and squeezed till the breath rushed from the human's lungs. The detective felt himself losing consciousness. It was impossible to break that steel grip—

Once more the fangs gaped at his throat. Vanning summoned his waning strength. His left hand gripped the monster's lower jaw, his right hand the upper. Sharp teeth ripped his fingers. He did not feel them, nor the foul, gusting breath that blew hot on his sweating face.

He wrenched viciously, dragging the creature's mouth wide open—and wider yet!

A hoarse roar bubbled from the Swamja's throat. There was a sharp crack, and the malformed body twisted convulsively. The mighty arms tightened, nearly breaking Vanning's back. Then—they relaxed.

- 32 -

The Swamja lay still, his spine snapped.

Vanning staggered up, hearing a roaring in his ears. It wasn't imagination. Across the square, monstrous figures came racing, shouting harshly— Swamja, dozens of them!

"Vanning!" Hobbs' voice croaked.

On the ground, three figures were wrestling in a contorted mass—Zeeth and Hobbs and the remaining Swamja. The monster was conquering. His bulging eyes glared with mad fury. Great muscles stood out on his gnarled arms as he tore at his opponents.

With a choking curse Vanning snatched up the gun his late enemy had dropped and sprang forward. His aim was good. The Swamja's eyes went dull as the destroying charge short-circuited his nerves.

The racing Swamja were dangerously close as Vanning bent, tearing at the monster's mighty hands. Useless!

He pressed his gun-muzzle into the Swamja's arm-pit and fired and fired again. Presently one arm writhed free. Vanning seized the two men, literally tore them from the creature's grip.

"The port!" Vanning gasped. "Get into—the ship!"

Hobbs lifted Zeeth and staggered around the bow. As Vanning turned to follow, he saw the slim body of Lysla lying motionless on the ground, in the path of the racing Swamja.

He sprinted forward, scooped up the girl in one motion, and swerved back, running as though all hell were at his heels. A croaking yell went up. Sickening pain lanced through Vanning, and he nearly fell. But the shock, though agonizing, wasn't permanent. Legs afire, the detective rounded the ship's bow and saw a circular hole gaping in the corroded hull.

Vanning sprinted forward, scooped up the girl, swerved back, and fired the full blast of his gun into the screaming face of the first Swamja.

He flung himself toward it. Through a crimson mist the masked face of Callahan swam into view. The man leaped out of the ship, caught up Lysla from Vanning's arms, and scrambled with her back through the port.

As Vanning tried to follow, he saw Callahan crouching on the threshold of the valve, an odd hesitancy in his manner. One of Callahan's hands was on the lever that would close and seal the ship. For a brief eternity the eyes of the two men met and clashed.

Vanning read what was clear to read. If Callahan closed the port now, leaving Vanning outside—he would be safe from the law. No doubt the man knew how to pilot a space-ship—

A shout roared out from behind Vanning. Callahan snarled an oath, seized the detective's hand, and yanked him into the ship. As a Swamja tried to scramble through the valve, Callahan's foot drove viciously into the monster's hideous face, sending him reeling back among his fellows.

Then the port clanged shut!

The port clanged shut, and the sudden silence of the ship was nerve-shattering in its instant cessation of sound.

Vanning managed to get to his feet. He didn't look at Callahan. Lysla, he saw, was still motionless. Hobbs was kneeling beside her.

"Lysla—she all right?" the detective rasped.

"Yes." Hobbs managed a weak grin. "She got in the way of a paralyzing charge—but she'll be all right."

"Okay." Vanning turned to the controls. They were archaic—in fact, the whole design of the ship was strange to him. It had been built a century ago, and rust and yellow corrosion was everywhere.

"Think it'll blast off?" Callahan asked as Vanning dropped into the pilot's seat.

"We'll pray! Let's see how much fuel—" He touched a button, his gaze riveted on a gauge.

The needle quivered slightly—that was all.

Callahan didn't say anything. Vanning's face went gray.

"No fuel," he got out.

There was a clanging tumult at the port, resounding from the outer hull.

"They can't get in," Callahan said slowly.

"We can't raise the ship," Vanning countered. "When we've used up all the air in here, we'll suffocate. Unless we surrender to the Swamja."

Hobbs gave a croaking laugh. "Not likely. There aren't any weapons here. The ship's been stripped clean."

Callahan said, "If we could break through the dome—"

"There might be enough fuel for that—if it hasn't deteriorated. But then what? We'd crash. Certain death. You know that."

Vanning clicked another button into its socket. "Let's see if the visi-plate works."

It did. On a panel before him a dim light glowed. It gave place to a picture, clouded and cracked across the middle. They could see the square, with the Swamja swarming into it in ever-increasing numbers, with the twisted buildings rising in the background, and the tower-tube shining far away.

Vanning caught his breath. "Listen," he said. "There's still a chance. A damned slim one—"

"What?"

The detective hesitated. If he took time to weigh this mad scheme, he knew it would seem utterly impossible. Instead, he snapped, "Brace yourselves! We're taking off for a crash landing!"

Callahan looked at Vanning's set, haggard face, and whirled. He picked up Lysla's limp body and braced himself in a corner. Zeeth and Hobbs did the same. Before any of them could speak, Vanning had swung the power switch.

He was praying silently that there was still a little fuel left in the chambers, just a little, and that it would still work. His prayer was answered instantly. With a roaring thunder of rocket-tubes the life-boat bulleted up from the ground!

The bellow died. There was no more fuel.

Vanning stared at the visi-plate. Beneath him the city of the Swamja was spread, the elfin lights glimmering, the coral palaces twisted like strange fungus growths. Automatically his hands worked at the corroded guide-levers that controlled the wind-vanes on the ship's hull.

The space-boat circles—swept around—

The shining tower-tube loomed directly ahead. Jaws aching, teeth clenched, Vanning held steady on his course. The ship thundered down with wind screaming madly in its wake.

The tube loomed larger—larger still. It blotted out the city. One glimpse Vanning had of the metal surface rising like a wall before him—

And the ship struck!

Rending, ripping, tearing, the space-boat crashed through the tube, bringing it down in thundering ruin. Briefly the visi-plate was a maelstrom of whirling shards. Then the glare of an elf-light raced up to meet the ship.

It exploded in flaming suns within Vanning's brain. He never knew when the ship struck.

V

He looked up into Zeeth's eyes. Blood smeared the Venusian's fat face, but he was smiling wanly.

"Hello," Vanning said, sitting up.

Zeeth nodded. "The others are all right. Still unconscious."

"The crash—"

"Hobbs has a broken arm, and I cracked a rib, I think. But the ship's hull was tough."

Vanning stood up. His eyes was caught by the movement on the visi-plate, which had incredibly survived the shock of landing. He moved forward, bracing himself against the back of the pilot's chair.

The city of the Swamja lay spread beneath him. The ship had lodged itself high on one of the towers, smashing its way into a sort of cradle, and then rolling down till its bow faced north. In the distance the jagged metal of the tube stood up forty feet above ground level. The rest of it wasn't there, though gleaming, twisted plates of metal lay here and there in the streets.

And through the avenues shapes were moving. They were the Swamja, and they moved like automatons. They moved in one direction only—away from the ship.

As far as Vanning could see the Swamja were pouring through their city.

Zeeth said softly, "You are very clever. I still do not understand—"

Vanning shrugged, and his voice was tired. "The only way, Zeeth. I broke the tube that shot the North-Fever virus into the upper air. The virus was released within the city, in tremendous quantity. You know how fast it works. And in this strength—"

"Yes. It strikes quickly."

"Once you've had the fever, you're immune to it ever afterward. So the slaves won't suffer. Only the Swamja. They're getting a dose of their own medicine."

"They go north," Zeeth said. "Out of the city."

It was true. Far in the distance, the Swamja were pouring toward the north gate, and vanishing through the open valves there. Nothing could halt them. The deadly virus they had created was flaming in their veins, and—they went north.

The did not walk; they ran, as though anxious to meet their doom. Through the city they raced, grotesque, hideous figures, unconscious of anything but the terrible, resistless drive that drew them blindly north. Through the north gate, into the pass—

Through the pass—to the lava pits!

Vanning's shoulders slumped. "It's nasty. But—I suppose—"

"Even the gods must die," Zeeth said.

"Yeah.... Well, we've work to do. We'll get food, water, and supplies, and head south for Venus Landing to get help. A small party will do. Then we can commandeer troops and swamp-cats to rescue the slaves from this corner of hell. We can get through to Venus Landing all right—"

"Yes, that will be possible—though difficult. Vanning—" Zeeth's eyes hooded.

"Yeah?"

"Callahan is not here."

"What?"

The Venusian made a quick gesture. "He awoke when I did. He told me to say that he had no wish to go to prison—so he was leaving."

"Where to?" Vanning asked quietly.

"Venus landing. He left the ship an hour ago to get food and weapons, and by this time he is in the southern swamps, well on his way. At the Landing, he said, he would embark on a space-ship heading—somewhere."

"I see. He'll reach the Landing before we do, then. Before we leave, we'll have to get things in some sort of order."

Both Hobbs and the girl were moving slightly. Presently they would awaken—and then the work would begin. With the city emptied of the Swamja, it would be easy to organize the slaves, get up a party to march to Venus Landing—

Vanning's mouth twisted in a wry smile. So Callahan was gone. He wasn't surprised. Callahan would never know that the detective had awakened from the crash before any of the others—and had shammed unconsciousness till the fugitive had had time to make good his escape.

Vanning shrugged. Maybe he was a damn fool. Getting soft-hearted....

"Okay," he said to Zeeth. "Let's get busy. We've got a job ahead of us!"

- 40 -